Tales from the Temple

조오현

Cho Oh-hyun

CODHILL PRESS
FORSYTHIA

CODHILL PRESS

New Paltz, New York *www.codhill.com*

FORSYTHIA

THIS IS A CODHILL BOOK

Codhill books are published by David Appelbaum for Codhill Press.

ISBN 978-1-949933-02-4
First Edition

This publication was made possible in part by the generous
support of the Manhae Foundation.

Cover photograph courtesy of *Pixabay.*

Book design by Bo-Leaf Studio.

In memoriam
Manak Musan Cho Oh-hyun

萬嶽 霧山 曺五鉉

아제아제 바라아제 바라승아제 모지사바하
아제아제 바라아제 바라승아제 모지사바하
아제아제 바라아제 바라승아제 모지사바하

Gate gate paragate parasamgate bodhi svaha

CONTENTS

KARMA! YOUR HOUSE IS ON FIRE!

Shortly after dawn, after the first service had ended, the old fire stoker at our temple got up as he always did, all the joints in his arms and legs cracking, and squatting in front of the stove of the huge meditation hall, he stoked the heating fire. "It looks like the head monk stayed out last night again," he said. "Why's there no sign of him?"

The old stoker would talk to himself all day as he made his rounds, thoroughly sweeping every corner of the temple. "Those stones in that heavenly stone bridge at Tongdosa Temple at Yangsan, those huge stones that even ten stout men couldn't move with all their strength combined—who do you think picked them up and carried them there? Anybody know? My grandfather got them from the arms and legs of the Maitreya at Iksan and hauled them in the middle of the night all by himself. That main crossbeam at Pyochungsa Temple in Miryang—who do you think carried *that* there? My grandfather carried it there! He broke his back while he was hefting that thing, I mean, even the A-frame carrier broke! And from that day he suffered a long time 'til he met his fate. When he died, he hugged me. He held me in his hands like tree bark, and he said 'Listen to the monks, boy. If you get hungry you can fill your belly with pine bark.' And he died. We wrapped his body tight in winding sheets and put him in the wood pile at the cremation grounds. The monk who scraped the match and lit the fire shouted out, '*Karma*, your house is on fire! *Karma*, your house is on fire! *Karma*, your house is on fire!' The woodpile was a mass of flames by then, but when the monk said that, it shuddered. Yes, it *shuddered*. My father took after my grandfather so he was strong as an ox. He wouldn't be full even after he ate ten bowls of rice, but he was afraid the monks would send him away for eating too much, so he always filled his belly with water. These days there's lots of food, but why not in those days? Anyway, why's the head monk not back yet? Is he sick or something?"

That's the sort of thing the old stoker would mumble throughout the day. These things they call "tales from the temple"—if you air them out—they just make the world needlessly deep and tangled. Not much more to say that's news.

THE SEAGULLS & THE EAST SEA

It happened some time ago. There was an elderly man, not especially holy-looking, but with a certain grace to his old age. He was sitting across from Mt. Nakson, on the very end of cliff that faces it, a dizzying and precarious place. He was sitting astride a rock all day, looking out at the waves on the surface of the East Sea.

I asked him, "Where are you from, old man?"

He said, "I'm sure I saw two seagulls flying over the horizon this morning, but they don't seem to be coming back." It sounded like he was talking to himself.

The next day he was at that same spot again, sitting in that same pose, so I asked him, "Did the two seagulls return?"

He said, "The sea was crying yesterday, but today it's not."

TWO SQUIRRELS

This isn't a legend or a story from a once upon a time, it happened just this past year at the hermitage where the nuns come to study. It's deep in the woods, that hermitage. You step into the courtyard, where the foundation stone is buried amongst the trees and the thousand-year-old pagoda is leaning—you can hear the sound of flowing water, and the cry of the black cuckoo permeates your clothes like ink. In the farthest corner of that courtyard there was a stone Buddha, and the devoted women who came to bear sons for the Dharma used to scrape and eat its nose—half of it was eaten away by them. So when you laughed, it looked like the stone Buddha was crying, and when you were actually crying, then it looked like it was laughing. Well, that desolate hermitage might just as well not have been there, but there was an abbess who had lived there for twenty years. Late that fall, she was standing by the stone Buddha holding onto the reflection of a branch that was floating downstream in the water. She saw two squirrels with acorns in their mouths busily going in and out of a stone wall. She said to herself, "*Aha!* There must be lots of acorns in that wall. We can make an offering of acorn jelly to the Buddha and then eat some ourselves. *Namu Amita Buddha.*" When she knocked down the stone wall, a good bushel of acorns did, indeed, come out of there. But after she got that bushel, she took every last one of the remaining acorns, made jelly, and ate it. The next morning she saw those two poor squirrels chewing on her white rubber shoes. They say those squirrels died eating those white rubber shoes.

IDIOT

A few days ago I was asked to give a talk at a company regarding Buddhism and economy. So I went and addressed an audience of about a thousand employees.

"Ladies and gentlemen!" I said. "In modern times there was a follower of the Dharma, a monk named Hyeweol (慧月慧明, 1862-1937). One winter, he called the people of the village together and had them level a hill to make a field for planting. But by and by, over the course of that winter, they were only able to level two acres, though the labor that went into it was equal to the time it would have taken to tend ten acres. The monk at the temple who was in charge of land management was angry, and he let it fly. '*Hyeweol!* Did you have to throw away *ten* acres of farmland for the sake of *two?*' Hyeweol replied, 'You're an idiot. Can't you see the ten acres are still right there and now we've created two more? I made good use of the villagers' time. Where else in the world is there profit like this? I'm going to do this again next winter.'"

At this point in my talk, the thousand employees in the audience laughed so hard their bellies shook. And the sound of that laughter from those people was unearthly, though I must admit I was having a belly laugh, too, myself.

A GARMENT

Zhenzhou Puhua (鎮州普化, 770-840/860), a Chan monk during the Tang Dynasty, made a plea one day. He said, "I need somebody to donate an article of clothing for me."

The temple-goers who heard him, both men and women, bought clothes and took them to him with heartfelt devotion. But Puhua only shook his head. "That's not it," he said. "I have no need for these clothes, so take them back." And he faced away and turned his back to them.

Hearing this news, Master Linji Yixuan (臨濟義玄, d. 866) nodded to himself. And then he had a carpenter quickly make a coffin and took it to Puhua's dwelling. "Here," he said. "I had this new garment prepared for you." And only then did Puhua beam with joy.

THE MOON IN THE WATER

It was nighttime and everyone else was sleeping. Under the calm moonlight, the tree branches cast mottled patterns against the pale skin on the paper doors of the temple rooms. Mr. Kim—a lay Buddhist student who was pondering the question, "What is the self?"—couldn't get to sleep, and so he had come out into the courtyard. He walked for a while there, treading through the sound of wind chimes that seemed to carry no more than knee-high from the ground. That's when he saw the stranger sitting there, at the edge of Gwaneum Pond, with his arms hugging his knees to his chest. "In the middle of the night?" Kim thought. Even as his hair stood on end, something made him go and stand behind the young man and keep a watchful eye. Perhaps the man sensed Kim's presence, perhaps not—he just stared at the deep, mysterious reflection of the moon floating on the water. He sat there, not moving, like some hastily-packed bundle of baggage. Just then, the moon shifted, drawing up its own shadowy reflection, and a misty drizzle began to come down. The stranger stood up on his feet as if he were a weak, old man. "Well, I'll be..." he said. "You can look at the moon in the water but you can never scoop it out...."

Kim watched him rub his hands over his haggard face and stagger out of the temple gates as dawn was breaking.

A GLAD & HAPPY & GOOD DAY

They say that on the day of his death, Linji Yixuan (臨濟義玄, d. 866) was having a leisurely old-fashioned tea with his attendant when he said, "…it is not strange to die while sitting, nor is it so wonderful to die standing. And to die standing on your head isn't all that impressive, is it? I'll just have to go like this."

He got up from his seat, went out into the courtyard, stood a moment, took one step, two steps, three, four, five, six, seven steps. And then, still apparently in mid-stride, he died right on that spot.

This anecdote was told to the old hall monitor at our temple whose job it is to keep monks awake by hitting them with the warning stick if they nod off during meditation. When he heard this he laughed bitterly and, revealing his buck teeth, he said, "As I live, it seems to me that the most glad and happy and good day in all this world is the day you die."

CLOSE YOUR EYES TO SEE THE SPIRIT

Twenty or so years ago, while I was on the road to Gyerimsa Temple in Geumreung, I met a stonemason. He looked to be about fifty, and he was on a huge boulder on the side of the path, marking out ink lines and tapping in little cleats. People were standing around, asking, “What are you making?” But he didn’t answer, and went on as if he hadn’t heard. Several years passed, and I was going back to Gyerimsa on some business when I saw that the boulder had been transformed into a Maitreya Buddha so realistic it looked like it was about to open its golden mouth. And the stone beside it had become a stone lion lamp lighting up the path. I was so shocked I stood there a long time, unable to move. Then, one day after another ten years or so had passed, I met the stonemason again by chance in Inner Seorak’s Baekdam Valley. I asked, “Are you still working with stone these days?” The old man was sitting hunched on a wide, flat rock. He was silent at first, and then, heaving a sigh, he said, “Master, it seems to me I’ve been walking around aimlessly my whole life. All my life, to this day, I devoted to working with stone, but now that I’m seventy, I look back and see there’s more than seventy rocks I cracked, and they’ve all become Buddhas and they all need to be smashed. If I could’ve seen those

Buddhas with my eyes from the start, without those ink lines and those cleats, I would never have taken up my hammer in the first place...." He trailed off and just sat for a long time looking off into the distance. Then he said, "Master, this rock we're sitting on stretches out in the four directions and that bunch of stones in the water—close your eyes and quietly look at them. There are baby Buddhas playing inside. Over there, over on that side—the Buddha's face is in that stone wall. The boulder over there is a lotus lantern, and in front of it—that half-stone—is a Triyaka. To the left of that, there's the Bodhisattva Manjushri. When I was young, I couldn't see those figures even if I looked with my open eyes, and so I had to draw lines on the rocks.... But now my eyes are gone. It's easy for me to forget the path even when I've been on it before...I have to close my eyes to see the light of the spirit. If I just close my eyes I can see the Buddhas sitting inside the stone.... Just give it a tap, tap, and then it exists. Just give it a tap...." He went on like that, like someone keening, who has let go of himself, and then he said nothing more.

MASTER MANGONG

During the Japanese annexation, the Japanese Government General gathered all the head monks together from the thirty-three head offices in the country and announced to them, "We expect Korean monks to get married."

After a long silence, Master Mangong (滿空月面, 1871–1946) of Sudeoksa Temple replied, "One who violates the monastic rules cannot drink the water of that land and cannot tread upon its earth. Moreover, a monk who becomes an apostate will die and be reborn as an animal. The Government General in Joseon has surely become an animal in Hell." Thus, he sternly rebuked the Japanese program of cultural erasure.

Manhae Han Yong-un (萬海 韓龍雲, 1879-1944), upon hearing these words, ran, without a break, to see Master Mangong. Knocking on his window, he offered his praise: "With a lion's roar, you've shattered the demons' brain. And so it's done, but wouldn't a stick have worked even better than a shout?"

Master Mangong replied, "My naive friend, as a rule, a lion only shows its shadow."

AZALEAS

I'd heard that the lotuses were in bloom at Haeinsa Temple's White Lotus Hermitage, and so I went to see them. But all the white lotuses had closed by the time I got there, and instead a Zen Master was sitting cross-legged there, as if he were on one of the 10,000 Peaks of Kaya.

"Where have you come to?" he asked.

"...."

"Were you here once before?" he asked.

"...."

"Of what temple are you the abbot?" he asked.

"...."

For the life of me I just couldn't answer him. But as I was on my way back, I saw what I hadn't been able to see on the way there—the Heungryudong waterfall, in between some boulders. There was a patch of late azaleas with their roots dipping into the water, and they seemed to say, "Those who perished at the tip of that sharp tongue are more numerous than those who drowned in Haeinsa Temple's ocean of Tripitaka!" And there was all at once an explosion of scarlet water, as if it were the flowers shouting, and that water flowed, endlessly flowed, down toward the harbor at Heungryudong.

十一

THE TEARS OF AN UNFILIAL SON

One day Jeonghyu (正休, b. 1944) of Mt. Chiak called on the phone and told me the following story.

"A long time ago in China there lived a man who would become the famous monk Lu Chang (陸常). He had just come running out of the house, having gotten a thrashing from his mother. But a little while later, he went back inside. 'Mother, I'm terribly sad,' he said to her. He had tears in his eyes. His mother said, 'This is the first time I've seen you cry after mother's beating. You brat! Is it so sad to get a beating from your mother?' Lu Chang got down on his knees and said, 'Mother, it's not because of the beating that I'm crying. In the old days, my calves would be covered in purple bruises and I was in awful pain. But today you beat me for so long and yet it doesn't hurt. You've grown old, Mother. It seems you've lost your strength.' And he sobbed until his shoulders shook."

Here Master Jeonghyu paused for a moment. "How much is this story worth, do you think?" he asked.

"Old people, they speak straight to the outrageous truth," I said. "They transcend the workings of the normal mind. You can't weigh it or put a price on it and there's no middleman, either, to bargain with.

"And so, in this world, where there are actually rules and regulations and the like, where you have to bargain, the price is a million won."

Master Jeonghyu answered, "Very well."

I burst into laughter for a while. But when I put down the phone and listened, it wasn't laughter I heard. It was the tears of an unfilial son.

THE OLD BLACKSMITH

One day, when Master Gaong of Cheoneunsa Temple was in his temporary quarters, he told me, "Back when I was a young mendicant monk, I was in Jeolla Province in Gochang district near a street of metal workers. I happened to meet an old blacksmith there who was tempering steel.

"I asked, him, 'Are you making any money?' and the old blacksmith, not even looking up at me said, 'Yesterday, someone came and had some tools sharpened, and today I sold a few twelve-penny nails, and as you can see I am repairing a palanquin.' And so I didn't ask him anything else. I left. A few days after that, I went looking for him and again, I asked him, 'Are you making any money?' Then the old blacksmith said, 'This is a family business passed down for three generations…and *damn it*!' he spat. 'How could I forget the anniversary of my wife's death?!' Then he started pounding on lumps of fire." With that, Master Gaong went outside and stared off into the distance at the mountains.

"Are you thinking of going somewhere?" I asked him.

"I miss that old blacksmith," he said.

BULGUKSA TEMPLE

After worshipping at Bulguksa Temple I went looking for the East Sea, and what I found was that the ancient temple of a thousand years had followed me and was already reflected in the vast ocean.

Bulguksa, the thousand-year temple, reflected in the sea, and in the crystal-clear reflection of Bulguksa is the reflection of Manjushri, and in the reflection of Manjushri is reflected the Dharma of Emptiness, and in the reflection of the Dharma of Emptiness is reflected the bright light of the Realm of Beasts, and within the bright light of the Realm of Beasts is reflected the darkness of the Heavenly Realm, and in the darkness of the Heavenly Realm is reflected the Realm of Desire, and in the reflection of the Realm of Desire are reflected the gilded lotus petals of the River Jambu, and in the reflection of the gilded lotus petals of the River Jambu is reflected Indra's Net, and in the reflection of Indra's Net is the reflection of an eon, and within the reflection of an eon is reflected the Shakyamuni Pagoda, and in the reflection of the Shakyamuni Pagoda is reflected the Lotus Pond of Lost Love, and in the reflection of the Lotus Pond of Lost Love are the maidens of Asadal, the Morning Land, and in the reflection of the maidens of

Asadal, the Morning Land, are reflected more reflections, each to each different, and each reflection reflects every other, and even if one were to speak of them, considering the innumerable perils of such utterance, they cannot be described, however much one's desire—and all those reflections were taken up within my own.

After worshipping at Bulguksa Temple I went looking for the East Sea, and what I found was that the ancient temple of a thousand years had followed me and was already reflected in the vast ocean.

十四

NOW THAT THE PLUM IS RIPE

Among the many disciples of the venerable Chinese Chan master Mazu Daoyi (馬祖道, 709-788), there was one Damei (大梅, 752-893), whose name means "Great Plum."

When Damei first visited Master Mazu, he asked, "What is the Buddha?" To which Mazu answered, "What the mind is, the Buddha is."

Afterwards, Da Mei went by himself deep into the mountains. Many seasons passed, and Mazu quietly sent a monk to visit Da Mei.

"Whose disciple are you," the visitor asked.

"I am a disciple of Master Mazu."

"What did you learn from him?"

"He told me that what the mind is, the Buddha is," said Da Mei.

"Well, these days Master Mazu is saying something different about Buddha and mind. His teaching is 'Not mind, not Buddha.'"

"That old geezer stays on to confuse the world instead of dying," said Da Mei. "But as for me, it's still 'What the mind is, the Buddha is.'"

Hearing this report upon the monk's return, Master Mazu called together scores of his disciples and told them, "Now that the Plum is fully ripe, go to him and pluck and eat to your hearts' content."

THE DOG APRICOT

Two days after the beginning of last spring there was an old country man sitting hunched over at the base of the stupa at our temple. He looked to be at least eighty, and he was coughing and sipping loudly from a cup of soju.

Seeing the condition he was in, an old monk scolded him, "How dare you! If you drink here you'll end up in Hell. Go drink out there." Behind his glasses, his eyes were sharp and disapproving.

The old man, looking up at the monk, scrunched up his already wrinkled face and sucked on his cigarette until his cheeks went hollow. As he staggered out, he said, "They say there's no monk who doesn't stink in this temple. If I'd of known you monks would be rude to me when I got old, I would of just watched when the commies put Daeheung Temple to the torch back then. I worked my fingers to the bone, roasting in the rice paddies, in the threshing yard, working till I was bone tired, even when it was just sloppy empty heads of grain, just so you monks could do your studying. Never once did I ever resent it. Yeah, when the commies came when the war broke out, it looked like it was gonna be life or death for this place, and all you monks went looking for a safe hideout and you abandoned this place like it was an old beehive. Well, when the monsoons came in the summer, the stupa was collapsing and the racket of guns and airplanes made the tiles crack and the place was overgrown with weeds and rain was dripping down the pillars and the rafters. Then the time the commies were laying low and then they slaughtered all the cows and ate them and then when they left they set fire to the big beams. Who do you think put out the fire then? Who looked after the temple.... If one of you *monks* did that, he should step up right now. We folks put out the fire and repaired the broken walls and pulled up all kinds of weeds and farmed while we were at it. And then when you all came back from wherever you were hiding, we were all burnt dark by the sun and filthy and all elbows and ribs and skin and bones, us tenant farmers. And when you all called us here and told us to help repair the place, and even then we just rubbed our faces. Now I'm old like this and you monks have no respect. Throw me out? If I'd of known this back then, then I would of just had a great time watching this place burn down...."

So that old man spat out all these curses outside the Ilju gate and the dog apricot tree there heard and absorbed it all—to the point that it got sick. But to this year's spring visitors it showed the world's most radiant flowers. It presented us with the brightest smile in the world.

THE CRY OF WILD DUCKS

Master Mazu and his disciple Paichang were silently walking along a river bank at sunset when they saw a formation of wild ducks flying into the west where the evening sky was dyed red. Suddenly Mazu asked his disciple, "What is that noise?"

"It's the cry of the wild ducks," said Paichang.

They walked in silence for a while, and Mazu asked again, "Where has the cry of the wild ducks gone?"

"It has gone far off into the west," Paichang replied. But as soon as the words left his mouth, Mazu grabbed Paichang's nose and viciously twisted it.

Paichang screamed *"Ouch! Ouch!"* at the unexpected assault, whereupon Mazu roared like a thunderbolt, "You said it's flown away, but isn't it still here?"

Some time ago, after hearing this story, I asked Abbot Kyoengbong of Tongdosa Temple, "The flock of wild ducks had obviously flown away. Why did the teacher yell 'isn't it still here'?"

Abbot Kyeongbong clicked his tongue and said, "If you were a student, you'd say the cry of the wild ducks is still in the water. Since you're not a student, go have a look at the Buddha floating under the stone bridge. The world you see and hear is inexhaustible, but you'll want to know that the world you can't see or hear is infinite, too.... *Tsk. Tsk. Tsk.*"

MASTER MUSTA' LEFT THE MOUNTAIN

When a fellow monk from Hancheonsa Temple visited me with some prominent poets from Seoul, I showed them Naerin Stream and the Eoseongjeon house in South Seorak, and then we went to an inn and sat at a table from which we could see the Jumunjin beach along the East Sea, the foamy waves, and the gulls in the sky like water. The barmaid, whose plain looks belied her wide-ranging culinary skill, served us tasty side dishes—spiced clam made in rice water, dried halibut pounded and torn into little strips—and then there was an assortment of freshly-caught items, a flounder with scales and fins removed, cut open while still alive, all its flesh exposed, served with the bones and head and set up on the platter as if were in a drunken sleep; and even so, though it was all going into the guests' mouths, this fish, all mouth and eyes and bones, blinked its eyes and opened and closed its mouth as if it were alive and had something to say—or maybe nothing to say at all, this flounder served raw along with squid, and halibut, and sea urchin, and sea cucumber, a combination of raw seafood dishes made from all of these spread on the table with a few bottles of soju, the people sitting all around. "This seafood sure is fresh," they said. "We never see the likes of it in Seoul." And as the words came out of their mouths the food went in, and the liquor went in, and as the first two bottles of soju were emptied, out came the talk of life, nature, literature, philosophy, and religion, seeming to go on for ages, and then once four bottles, then five bottles, were emptied, up and down went the names of famous figures in politics and religion and literature, and then professors, and they were thoroughly chewed over, just like the raw seafood, and as they happened to be the world's leading poets they were like the croaking of a lone frog on a moonlit spring night piercing the cosmos, and as they had begun they made it their duty to cover the whole of it until they arrived at all times and all places, the endless ocean—they lifted it all and put it all down, chattering and laughing, and as they got up from their places at the table, that flounder had finally closed its eyes and shut its mouth, and...

...*damn*, the story actually begins here, if I'm to tell it properly, as we came out of the tavern and walked a ways, we met an old fisherman who must have had a drink or two somewhere, because he approached me so matter-of-factly and asked, in common speech, "Excuse me, but how long's it been since you became a monk?" So I answered him the same way, in common speech, "It's been about forty years," and I had a look at him, and whether it was because he was so happy or because it happened to be the anniversary of a death, the old fisherman's sunburnt face got flushed, like the red tide appearing on the deep blue sea, and he said, "Then Master musta' left the mountain." And as he came a step closer, one of the distinguished poets from Seoul stepped in front of him, blocking his way, saying, "Look here, old man, you can't speak so rudely to the Abbot! Why would he have left his mountain?" and his tone was grave, and the red tide on the old man's face receded, as if the ocean had slowly taken it back, and he said, "I'm old...I'm sorry, I misspoke to you distinguished guests...I heard you all talking about the endless ocean a little while ago...and, well, I held the tiller of a boat for over thirty years, and then I abandoned the old ways, so I had to say something, and what you heard..." and he said, "flocks of birds flying in the sky..." and "a season of bad catches..." and he walked away muttering to himself, just like that. That image. That was it.

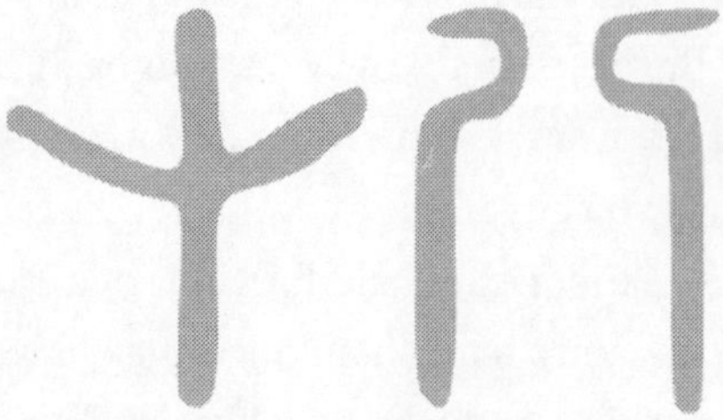

HOW MUCH DOES THIS SOUND WEIGH?

Su Dongpo (蘇東坡, 1037-1101) was a famous intellectual and writer during the Song Dynasty. They say that when he heard of the great Buddhist monk Cheng Hao, Su Dongpo put on a disguise and went to test him. And this is what ensued:

Cheng Hao spoke first. "Honored official, what is your name?"

"My surname is Cheng," Su Dongpo answered.

"Cheng, you say?"

"Do you mean to tell me that a renowned Buddhist master such as yourself fails to recognize the scales that are here to assess you?"

Su Dongpo's contemptuous words had only just left his mouth when Cheng Hao let loose a thunderous, "*Aaaaaahhhkk!*" And then, afterwards, he asked calmly, "Then how much does this sound weigh?"

Seriously humiliated at that moment, the crestfallen Su Dongpo returned, and his mind all shaken up, he composed the following *gatha:*

The mountainscape is, as it is, the Dharmakaya;
The sound of water is, as it is, the Buddha's teaching.

THE FISH MARKET AUNTIE

The great Master Seolbong (1890-1969) lived his whole life owning only one set of clothes and a staff. In his later years at Busan's Beomosa Temple, before his death, he had stopped eating meat but still enjoyed drinking rice wine.

One day he was at Busan's famous fish market, a place babbling with dialect and bustling with people, everything permeated with the smell of fish. He was stepping through the fishy mud when he caught the blinking eye of an old "auntie bodhisattva" who was slicing up a fresh fish on her counter with a thick-bladed knife. When she saw him she propped herself on her knees to straighten her back, and through her snaggletooth, she said, "They say nobody's seen even Master's nose these days. They say maybe you didn't wanna live in this world anymore and hauled off to Nirvana. Well, for the life of me, as I live today, I'm seeing you...."

She went up to Master Seolbong and grabbed his wrists, wrapping her fingers around them like a net. She wiped her eyes with the hem of her skirt, and then she took a crisp new 10,000 won note and slipped it in a white envelope. She put it into his pocket and, looking him right in the eye, said, "My second daughter-in-law's girl—she still isn't pregnant...I can't sleep. My second son got discharged from the army and got a job just so he could repay you for all your sacrifice and devotion...and so you could have a cup of rice wine. Could you please ask the Chilseongnim, the god of the seven stars, to bless us with a healthy, moon-faced boy? Well, even if he's a weakling, things being how they are?"

Master Seolbong looked inside the white envelope and decided to make it an occasion for a Buddhist teaching. "Auntie! Do you even *know* how much a little calf costs these days?" he said. "Do you? No? What about a little a piglet? They say a really plump one is worth a few 10,000 won bills these days. And you think *this* is enough to get you all a little boy?"

Another young auntie who was selling fresh squid in the stall across the way saw all this and couldn't help herself. She'd tried to keep from laughing, but she burst, and she laughed so long and hard her bottom got all wet. And a sea gull that had come scavenging happened to hear the sound of that laughter, and it must have flown far out over the ocean, spreading the news far and wide....

Because several years passed, and during Master Seolbong's funeral hundreds of sea gulls flocked at Busan's ocean front imitating the sound of the aunties crying—*sob sob sob*...and they cried and cried on, shedding tears drop after drop.

THE BELL-RINGER

At every 3 a.m. the bell-ringer at our temple would ring the massive bell, which must have weighted at least a thousand pounds. Once, I said to him, "They say the cold morning wind is bad for your health. What would you think of taking on a different job?"

"No, I can't," he replied. "I am going to ring this bell for Master Nodeok's passage to Nirvana. Twenty years ago, I rang the final bell for Master Josil's passing, and that sound—it rang out so pure and so loud and so long.... There was no one who didn't cry when they heard that bell.

"But since then I haven't once *ever* heard a sound like that. No matter how skillfully I use the ringer to strike this bell, I can't make it make that sound. Maybe the bell itself knows something? I don't know, but when it's time for Master Nodeok to enter Nirvana I think that sound will come again.

"Anyway," he said, "if I could just hear that sound one more time, then I can quit."

And so he continued being the bell-ringer, a job that no one else wanted.

二十一

THE MAN WHO FORGOT HIS SELF

A scholar from the country got to stay a night at the temple, and to show his appreciation he went to the quarters of the head monk to say goodbye. This is what he said:

"The general Lu Aigong asked Confucius, 'I heard that an absent-minded man who was moving forgot his wife and left her behind in the old house. How could that be?' Confucius replied, 'But that is not a serious man. A serious man will even forget his own self.'" After letting that sink in for a moment, the scholar asked, "In Buddhism, what sort of person would you say is one who forgets his own self?"

Many of the senior monks probably thought this was some sort of koan. They couldn't figure it out and stayed silent, but a one monk named Pilgrim Kim, who had hardly been at the temple for a month, spoke up.

"That would be someone just like you," he said, scolding the scholar. "That's what we mean by a man who's forgotten his self!"

After the country scholar left, abashed, the monk asked if he had behaved properly in rebuking the man. "I behaved rudely and thoughtlessly in front of you, too,

Master," he said. "I forgot myself, but didn't that Confucian scholar do the same?"

And then he closed his mouth tight and kept it that way.

THE UNDERTAKER & THE MONK

I went to make a condolence call after receiving the news that a dear fellow monk had died, and I happened to arrive while an old undertaker was preparing the body. He was meticulous to the last detail, like a traditional doctor diagnosing a patient's pulse. Not a square inch of the body was neglected, and after the body was all dressed there was an expression in the old undertaker's eyes, of wanting to give the departed a final embrace, as if what he had done was not enough, until finally he closed the lid of the coffin on the smell of death.

To be sure, if a family member—living under the same roof just this morning—were to die, we'd call that person a corpse. And when we hear that word, "corpse," we're covered in gooseflesh and don't want to go near. But here was a stranger he'd never seen before in his life, moreover an old man who died of a sickness, whose body was crawling with insects, and the undertaker was treating his body with such tenderness.

It was the first time I had witnessed something like this. Now that it was time for him to go and make his rounds paying his respects to the mourners in their mourning attire, I stopped him and asked, "How long have you been an undertaker?"

"I started when I was thirty-two," he said. "So it must be going on forty years now."

"Then you must have dressed a lot of bodies. Do you prepare other people's bodies this way?"

"What do you mean?" he said. "Living people are all different, but corpses—man or woman, of whatever age—well, they don't have different melting points, so to speak.

"When I was younger I did this for the money, but after hundreds of people a year, I realized at some point that I cared about my work. It was unexpected. People say they're afraid of the dead, but I'm afraid of the living. The dead are like my family these days, and sometimes I feel like I'm seeing my own dead body...."

At this point he bore an expression, as if he'd realized what he was saying sounded preposterous and he should stop talking.

But then, he said, "Well, I've gotten started, so let me ask you something. In my line of work I get to meet a lot of monks, and some tell me a man's body is just a container, a skin bag full of blood and puss. Since it's just a leather sack and a bundle of desire that was thrown away, then it's like the moon reflected in the water and the soul has no obstruction. That's good, they tell me.

"And then some monks tell me that the empty body that's like a scarecrow will soon be enlightened. And then, some monks just chant prayers for going to Nirvana after death....

"You monks must all have your own separate dogmas. But could you put that all aside for a moment and tell me the real truth? When we die, is there a Heaven and a Hell?

"I'm saying this after I've been an undertaker for a long while. This man's soul will go to Heaven, that one's will go to Hell. I feel that sometimes, so I'm just telling you. And this is something I say that might seem farfetched, but it's something I'm sure of. The body—I may see it for the first time—but according to that body, that person, I can tell if they had a pure and simple life. Or whether this old man had a generous heart or whether he purposely did things that he shouldn't have done, or whether this body is someone who only suffered in life or if this one had to live with false accusations....

"What do they say? A feeling? Intuition? The traces of a man's life are left on the body."

It seemed he was done then. He was silent. And though his strength was waning and he was old, perhaps he read in me something that said I wanted to hear more.

He continued: "Stonemasons, when they snap down the line and tap in the cleats, they put their soul into the rock. They say a metalworker is like that, too. But for me, the man who was breathing along with me this morning, is on his way to his final resting place....

"In any case, I couldn't do this work if my heart wasn't in it, but what happens when I put my heart in it? Sharing it with the dead? Will my life energy spill over into that corpse? It seems that way to me in the end, and it puts my mind at ease.

"Yes, it puts my mind at ease in the end. But to other people's eyes it looks like I'm doing it for the sake of the departed. But still, I...."

He looked at me for a moment. "I'm telling you something you already well know," he said, finally. "Me, too. When I was young, the Master from the temple on the mountain back there said I was fated to become a monk.

“But as you must know, I had some of what you call *karma* left over…and now I’m just a body, and all that’s left is to leave this world and be departed myself.”

And that is how he cast a pall over his final words.

二十三

MASTER SEOSAN

At Yeomjeon, a lay Buddhist scholar, whom I didn't know, asked me if I was a teacher at the temple. So I told him the following story:

The light on the water—the Master's clear eyes,
The mountain light—the Buddha's clear brow;
The moon is the root of the one mind
And the clouds are ever the scriptures.

When he was young, a monk named Soyo, who wrote this Zen poem, went looking for the great Master Seosan (西山大師, 1520-1604) to learn about the Dharma from him. But Master Seosan taught him only five lines of scripture a day, and that so irritated Soyo that he considered leaving.

On the same day he was having those second thoughts, Soyo happened to step out from studying for a moment. When he returned, he saw Master Seosan reading a grimy little book, which he then quickly tucked back in his inside pocket. This happened not just once or twice, but many times a day, each time Soyo left the room. Now Soyo was so full of curiosity and suspicion about Master Seosan that he could not leave.

One night while Master Seosan was asleep, Soyo used the opportunity to get a look at that little book without the Master's knowledge. But the old monk woke up instantly, as if he had been frightened out of his wits, and hid the book away even more carefully. The next day, Soyo was determined to leave. But when he went to say goodbye, Master Seosan threw the book at him, saying, "If you're going to leave, then at least take the book with you."

Soyo walked for a long time. Finally, he sat down under a tree, and with eyes full of curiosity he slowly opened the book and saw a Zen poem.

O thou fool who rides the ox in search of the ox,
Tomorrow, as you sit under a shadeless tree,
All will be extinguished like bubbles in the sea.

Soyo read this poem again and again and his suspicion about Master Seosan grew even deeper. He turned around and went back to the temple to ask the meaning of that poem, but in the meantime Master Seosan had attained Nirvana, leaving only his corpse behind. It was upon seeing that corpse that Soyo attained his first great awakening.

As the story came to an end, the lay scholar observed, "I see it's very hard being a teacher," and with that he walked outside.

二十四

NOT LINGERING IN THE MIND

They say Takuan Sōhō (沢庵宗彭, 1573-1645) of the Japanese Rinzai sect always looked like a dry branch or cold rock. Once, a young man showed him a picture of a beautiful prostitute and asked him to write a poem in appreciation, watching his expression the whole time out of the corner of his eye.

Takuan just gave a hearty laugh and wrote the following poem:

I sell the Buddha
She sells her body
Willows green, flowers red…
Each night, the moon
passes over the water,
Not lingering in the mind,
leaving no shadow behind

二十五

THE OTTER & THE HUNTER

A young hunter caught an otter that had come out to the water's edge in search of food and he skinned it and strutted home with its pelt, and the next day he noticed that the otter's bones—which he had thrown away—had left bloody tracks walking off, and so he cautiously followed the trail of blood into a cave, and inside the dark cave he saw the heap of the thin bones that was the mother otter he had skinned and flensed the day before still alive, and she was embracing her five tiny pups—which had not yet opened their eyes—and they couldn't see their mother's condition, and they were mewling for milk, and the hunter was as cruel as a man could be, but upon seeing the mother and her pups he could not help himself, and so he took the place of the mother otter until the pups were grown; he spent three years like that—which felt to him like three *kalpas*—entirely cutting off the paths of the world and the vagaries of the mind, and the only place someone like him could go after that was to a temple, and the temple refused him because of the gamey odor that exuded from his body, and so he stood in the yard with a brazier of burning charcoal on his head 'til the crown of his head exploded with a sound like a thunderclap, and only then did the head monk, whose name was Muwoe, heal his wounds with a special mantra, giving him a reason to live and—they say—bestowed upon him the name Hyetong. And all this happened during the reign of King Munmu (626-681) of Silla.

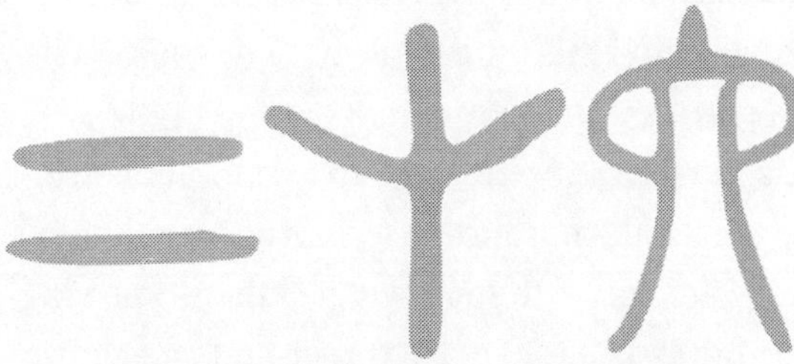

THE SAND PEAR FLOWER

In a remote valley on the way up to Deoksa Temple there's an old sand pear tree. It's rotted inside, its brittle branches are all broken, and its trunk pokes through a large rock. It stands in a shady spot, and so it blooms a little late, but when it's in full flower the sand pear's blossoms brighten the whole valley. So much so that the people who come looking for the temple see the tree first. When the grave-keeper of Doeksa Temple was a young man, he would see lots of those visitors. This is a story from those days.

The grave-keeper loved that sand pear and its flowers. When the bright petals fell from the branches or got blown down by the wind, they were sure to be stepped on. It seemed to him that there must be some place where those bright petals went, and so when he saw someone who looked they might know a thing or two, he would ask again and again. But never once did he get a good-enough answer.

Then, one year, a stout old man who'd taken the wrong path was sitting by himself in the shade of the blooming sand pear. "If it blooms it wilts, if it wilts it blooms," he was saying. "If I come I go, if I go I come…." He was all by himself, being happy and sad in turn. All this appeared a bit odd to the grave-keeper, who stood at a distance, watching this for a while until he couldn't help playing a prank on the old man.

The grave-keeper went right up to the old man, and standing practically nose-to-nose, he said, very loudly, "Old man! Old man! Are you saying all that—knowing where the flowers go to? Or are you just talking and you don't know?" Of course, the question was a joke, but somehow the grave-keeper must have aroused some hidden strength from an obscure corner of the old man's body. He hefted the maackia-wood staff he'd been holding and gave the grave-keeper a whack on the shoulders. It hurt so much the grave-keeper scooted off a little ways.

"You bastard!" said the old man. "The flowers go to the place where you run off to…as far…as much as it hurts where you got whacked by my stick…as far as that pain…that's where the flowers went! So go! Get lost!" And with that the old man went back to being happy and sad all by himself….

Starting the next year, when all the flowers of the sand pear had bloomed and fallen, there was one among the hundred someodd monks at Deoksa temple who knew where the flowers had gone—the grave-keeper—and once each of those monks had had his say, the whole year through, whether spring, summer, fall, or winter, the flowers of that tree bloomed, also brightening the hearts of the people.

That's the story.

二十七

A VERY GRACIOUS ANSWER

Goam Sangeon (古庵祥彦, 1899-1988), who was the third, fourth, and sixth Patriarch of Korea's Jogye Order stood up on the dais holding the scriptures, and after a moment, he recited the following:

There are oranges in the North
and tangerines in the South,
but in spring they produce
the same flowers.

And...

"One day when Changsha Jingcen (長沙景岑, 788-868) returned from a restful trip, a fellow monk said to him, 'Master, where have you been?'

'I'm returning from the mountains,' said Changsha.

'What mountains did you go to?'

'First I was in a valley lush with greenery, walking through the high grass, and then I slowly followed ridges thick with fallen blossoms, enjoying myself.'

The monk, his mouth agape, said, 'It sounds like everything is blooming!'

'It was certainly different from a withered lotus petal hanging in the cold winter sky,' said Changsha. 'The sunshine is good.'

Later, describing this conversation, the monk said that Changsha had given 'a very gracious answer.'"

Master Goam regarded the gathered monks, had a sip of tea, and commented:

Without ever stepping outside the house,
one can be in the wide world,
and without ever stepping indoors,
one can be forever inside a house.

And with this, he closed the scriptures and stepped down from the dais.

TREADING WATER

In the woods at noon
I hear a bird cry out.
On the shore, mid-morning,
I hear the gulls.
When will I hear the sound
of my own cry?

A few days ago a fellow monk, a mentor of mine from Haeinsa Temple, came and asked, "What are you doing these days?" so I wrote the above sijo and showed it to him.

"You lunatic!" he said. "I came thinking the bottle was tipped over, thinking it was empty, but the bottle is deeper than I thought. How long are you going to keep following the drum and not the Way? You're just treading water again!"

THE GREEN FROG

One morning, after lazily washing my face, I went over to the wall to dump out the water basin. A green frog happened to be sitting in the grass on the other side just at that moment and he got a terrible fright—*eek!* He leaped up—all the way up to the top of the wall—and alighted there as if he had slipped. As I saw him lying there panting, flat on his belly, I thought, *This guy is really something, he really is something!* I couldn't get over my admiration for him. But when I tried to compose a sijo poem with that green frog as the subject, I struggled day after day and only to fail in the end. I came to a minor realization: Whatever words I could come up with—for however many *kalpas*—to describe that frog, would never do him justice.

三十

THE OLD MONK & THE THIEF

When it comes to old temples, you find them where the mountains are high and the valleys are deep and the water is clear, where you see wobbly towers of stone, faded paintings of buddhas, abandoned stone lamps, old foundations with massive retaining walls, stone bridges, snow-damaged wood. They're in places that are a little chilly and windy, where at night you hear the sound of waterfalls and the cries of wild animals on the mountain, places where you need more quiet, but that isn't the case. It was a place like this, a hut where some old Taoist used to live and then abandoned, and so the walls were already in ruins and the yard was overgrown with grass and weeds. Well, an old monk named Ryōkan Taigu (良寛大愚, 1758–1831) appeared from somewhere and came to live in that hut. And when people in the nearby village found out they all came while he was away and repaired the walls, cut the grass, and pulled up the weeds. They fixed the place up all for his sake, but when Ryōkan returned, his reaction was lukewarm.

"You've pulled up all the grass," he said. "And now I can't even listen to the insects anymore."

Now, because his hut was in such good repair, a thief came, to burgle the place, thinking he must be rich. But Ryōkan had nothing, so he took off the clothes he was wearing and gave them to the thief. Ryōkan came out into the yard naked and, gazing up at the moon, he said, "How I wish I could have given him this beautiful moon."

三十一

SERMON

Master Goam mounted the dais, and holding his staff high, he said:

"One day the Shakyamuni Buddha sat on the high seat to give a sermon. But just at that moment, before the sermon had even begun, the bodhisattva Manjushri rapped the white staff, signaling that it was over. 'Observe carefully the dharma the Thatagatha reveals,' he said. 'The Buddha's teachings are like what you have just witnessed.' Then, presently, the Buddha himself came down from the high seat."

His sermon done, Goam looked around and put down his staff.

TRANSLATOR'S AFTERWORD

Buddhists like to think that a deceased monk, especially one who was renowned, will permanently enter Nirvana after this lifetime. But this may be a case of well-intentioned but wishful thinking. The Korean Buddhist tradition is Mahayana, and the goal of the Mahayana path is not simply to become an arhat and experience enlightenment for oneself, but to be a bodhisattva. That means a Korean monk has vowed that, upon reaching the very threshold of Nirvana, he will return to this world of dust and help *all other sentient beings* enter Nirvana before entering himself.

In translating these tales from the temple, it was impossible not to notice what appeared to be a preoccupation with death on Master Cho's part. Indeed, that theme permeates much of his poetry as a whole: mortality, death, the preparation for death, the aftermath of death. To a casual reader, especially from the west, this may appear to be a morbid fascination or a suggestion of fear, particularly the fear of the unknown that follows life; but in the Mahayana tradition this is a look forward to work yet to be accomplished, perhaps even an impatience to return, better-equipped, into a new incarnation of being of assistance to others. In the tradition of Buddhist poetry, the legacy of one's observations on such themes can serve to relieve karma, to be cautionary and edifying.

In remembrance of Master Cho's passing, it is especially fitting to recall that 2019 is also the 100th anniversary of the March 1st Movement, of which Master Cho's predecessor, the great Buddhist activist poet Manhae Han Yong-un (1879-1944), was a part. As I was translating this volume, I had repeatedly wondered why—of all possibilities with symbolic meaning—there were 31 entries. It perplexed me like a koan because, having immersed myself in Master Cho's work, I knew there would be layers of meaning there. Earlier, while writing the introduction to my translation of Kim Man-jung's *Kuunmong*, I had puzzled over the Buddhist numerology (the 5 skandhas, the 6 illusions, the 8-fold path, the 9 clouds, etc.), and it was perhaps this sort of engagement that made me realize what should have been the first obvious symbolism. The numbers 3 and 1, in Korean, are pronounced *sam* and *il*, which is what the March 1st movement is called: *Samil Undong*. A protest against the Japanese colonial authorities for Korea's *liberation*.

Likewise, the 31 story sijo in this collection are aimed at contributing to the reader's liberation—not from Japanese colonial rule, but from the "rule," the entrapments, of this world of dust. It is no accident that 3 and 1 ironically add up to 4 (*sa*), which in Korean sounds the same as the word for "death," which is what liberates us from this life. Indeed, in the Korean Buddhist tradition, *Samil Undong* takes on another resonance altogether. *Sam* (3) sounds very much like *salm* (to live)and *il* (1) sounds like *il* (work). *Undong*, which is translated as "movement" can also mean "exercise," or, in the Buddhist context, "practice." This means that *samil undong* can be read as "the practice of life's work." No surprise that it adds up to *sa*, or death. But in this context it is not a death to be feared, but to be returned to and from, to be entered temporarily with a legacy of teaching in a lineage of Buddhist poets. Master Cho very consciously participated in this lineage of poetry aimed at liberation.

And so, on this anniversary of Master Cho's passing, we also mark the 100th anniversary of those martyred at Pagoda Park during the 3.1 Movement as we read the words of Manak Musan in the lineage of Manhae. The traditional Korean exclamation, in this context, is *MANSAE!* which means to *live* for 10,000 years.

—Heinz Insu Fenkl
Pougheepsie, New York

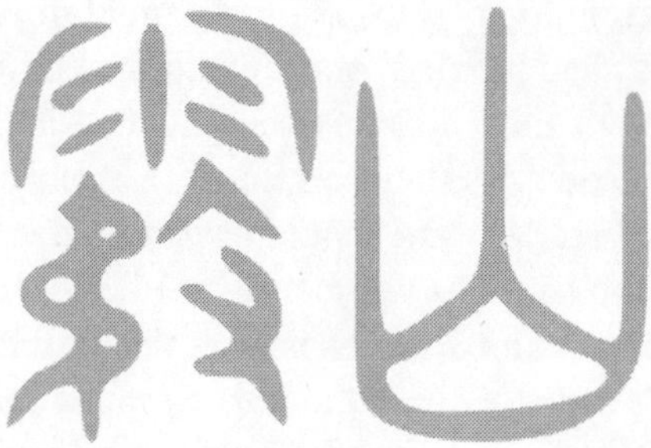

ABOUT THE AUTHOR

Cho Oh-hyun (1932–2018), who wrote under his Buddhist name *Musan*, was born in Miryang in South Gyeongsang Province of Korea. He lived in the mountains since he became a novice monk at the age of seven. Over the years he wrote hundreds of poems, including many in sijo form. Before his death, he was one of Korea's most prominent sijo poets. In 2007 he received the Cheong Chi-yong Literary Award for his book *Distant Holy Man*. Translations of his poetry have appeared internationally in numerous journals, including *Asymptote*, the *Buddhist Poetry Review*, *Asia Literary Review*, *AZALEA: Journal of Korean Literature & Culture*, *The Adirondack Review*, *Written River*, *The Shawangunk Review*, *Kyoto Journal*, *Tricycle: the Buddhist Review*, *Sijo: An International Journal of Poetry & Song*, and *World Literature Today*. A volume of his poems, *For Nirvana: 108 Zen Sijo Poems* was published by Columbia University Press in 2016.

ACKNOWLEDGMENTS

Many thanks to Kwon Youngmin and the Manhae Foundation for the funding that made this book possible. Thanks also to David Appelbaum of Codhill Press for taking on the project and bringing it into its current form. And special thanks to Bella Dalton-Fenkl for the logo-design and proofreading, and to Tiff Scott for proofreading and editorial feedback.

COLOPHON
κολοφών

This book was set in Minion Pro, part of the Minion family of typefaces designed by Robert Slimbach.

The archaic Chinese characters are from those compiled by Richard Sears for the Chinese Eytmology website (*www.hanziyuan.net*).

The enso above the table of contents is taken from the second syllable (오) of Master Cho's signature, which appears on the title page.

On back cover is *The Heart Sutra* text from a woodblock of the *Tripitaka Koreana.*